A-Z of **EDU**

CW00384328

By Brin Best

Cartoons:
Phil Hailstone

Published by:

Teachers' Pocketbooks
Laurel House, Station Approach,
Alresford, Hampshire SO24 9JH, UK
Tel: +44 (0)1962 735573
Fax: +44 (0)1962 733637
E-mail: sales@teacherspocketbooks.co.uk
Website: www.teacherspocketbooks.co.uk

*Teachers' Pocketbooks is an imprint of
Management Pocketbooks Ltd.*

© Brin Best 2003

This edition published 2003

ISBN 1 903776 52 X

British Library Cataloguing-in-Publication
Data – A catalogue record for this book is
available from the British Library.

Design, typesetting and graphics by Efex Ltd.
Printed in UK.

Contents

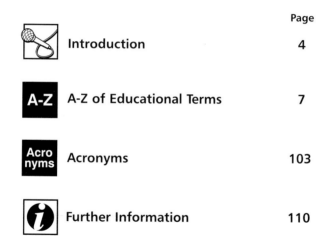

Introduction

This is the book I wish I'd had in my pocket throughout my teaching career. The state education system in England seems to attract more than its fair share of jargon and acronyms, which can be baffling to those at the chalkface.

The book is aimed at teachers who are new to the profession, as well as more established teachers and school managers who would like to keep up with the latest developments and initiatives. It will help you understand what you hear – from the conference to the staffroom – or read in government publications and the pages of the Times Educational Supplement. If you are a parent or carer of a child at school in England, there is much here for you too in helping you understand the system under which your child is being educated.

I have made the book specific to England as there are so many terms that relate to this country alone. No doubt there could be companion volumes for the Scottish, Welsh and Irish education systems.

In deciding what to include, I have tried to cover all the more general education terms and acronyms used regularly in primary and secondary schools in England in 2003. I have not delved deeply into specific subject areas, as this would have resulted in a much larger book and one that certainly would not fit snugly inside the pocket. I have also avoided many general words which are not restricted in their use to education settings as these definitions can easily be found in any good dictionary.

The aim has been to provide concise definitions by using the minimum of words, thereby keeping the book as user friendly as possible. I use website addresses extensively to signpost the reader to more detailed information.

Throughout my career working in and supporting schools, I have felt strongly that teachers should participate fully in the discussion about the key issues facing them and their students. Sometimes the jargon can get in the way and I hope this book can play a small part in demystifying the language surrounding the education system in this country.

A plea
The pace of educational change in England means that the book will inevitably need updating on a regular basis. You can play your part by alerting the publisher at info@teacherspocketbooks.co.uk to new terms and acronyms for inclusion in the next edition. If your suggestion is accepted you will be acknowledged in the book and receive a money-off voucher redeemable against your next purchase of a Teachers' Pocketbook.

Note: To save space I have taken the liberty of using the acronyms LEA for Local Education Authority, and DfES for the Department for Education and Skills throughout the book, as these are widely known to all teachers. For all other acronyms, first go to the section at the back to discover what the abbreviation stands for, then find the definition in the main text.

Acknowlegements

Several people have helped me improve the comprehensiveness, accuracy and accessibility of this book. These people have suggested words, checked entries or provided inspiration when I was finding difficulty constructing a concise definition.

I thank David Allen, Ros Baynes, Elaine Doxey, Linda Edge, Niki Elliot, Shirley Hayes, Kath Metcalfe, Peter Metcalfe, Sue Walton and Joanna Wells. Peter Metcalfe also provided valuable assistance proofreading. I would also like to thank Jane Knightsbridge-Randall who first helped me to see the importance of jargon busting, and the group of students with whom I worked on the environmental jargon busters all those years back.

While gratefully accepting the help others have given me, I am happy to accept any errors or omissions which remain, as my own responsibility.

Accelerated learning – Learning which proceeds at a faster rate, and with deeper understanding, than that normally expected using conventional teaching methods. In the last few years techniques and approaches have been developed, taking into account recent knowledge of how the brain works, that allow children to learn more effectively. These include *mind mapping, *multiple intelligences, knowledge of *learning styles and use of *thinking skills. Accelerated learning also includes the promotion of a positive learning environment, and ensures learners are in an appropriate physiological and psychological state to learn.

Acceleration – The process whereby more able children's education is fast-tracked by placing them in a higher year group, or entering them early for examinations.

A2 – The part of the *A-level examination taken after two years of study, mainly by students in year 13.

Ability – The capacity of a child to do something well compared with others of a similar age. *See also *less able and *more able*.

Access course – A course, often offered by *Further Education colleges, providing an alternative way to enter university for students who do not have the standard entry qualifications.

Accountability – Refers to the increasing trend for schools to have to justify how they are spending their funds.

Accreditation – The awarding of a certificate or units which count towards further professional development.

Accreditation of Prior Learning (APL) – The process whereby a person's previous achievements are taken into account when awarding a certificate.

Action plan – A plan which makes clear the steps that need to be taken to reach an intended goal. *See also *post-OFSTED action plan.*

Action research – Research concerned with the everyday practical problems of teachers, rather than educational theory. Action research is often carried out by teachers themselves.

Active learning – Learning which stimulates children to play an active part in the learning process.

Added value – *See *value added.*

Admission criteria – A means of allocating child places to schools which are over-subscribed. Individual schools often have their own admission criteria.

Advanced Extension Award – Extension examinations for post-16 children, introduced in 2002 in 17 subjects.

Advanced-level (A-level)(A2) – A qualification awarded to students, usually in Y13, who reach the pass mark in *AS and *A2 examinations combined. There are five grades ranging from A to E.

Advanced Level Information System (ALIS) – A *value-added monitoring system that identifies performance indicators for post-16 students.

Advanced Skills Teacher (AST) – An experienced teacher who is given an enhanced salary to work within and outside their main school to spread expertise and good practice. ASTs undergo a rigorous assessment and must gain approval from their school and *LEA to be granted their new status.

Advanced Subsidiary level (AS-level) – The component of the *A-level examination taken after one year of study, usually by children in year 12. Many students continue into a second year to complete the full *A-level. Others do not and are awarded an AS-level certificate and grade if they reach the pass mark. For university entry purposes AS-levels have half the value of the full *A-level.

Advanced Subsidiary Vocational Certificate of Education (ASVCE) – A post-16 vocational qualification which is more demanding than an ordinary *AS-level because it is assessed at the full *A-level standard.

Advanced Vocational Certificate of Education (AVCE) – A post-16 vocational qualification which replaced the Advanced GNVQ.

Adviser – An *LEA employee whose role is to help schools become more effective by working face to face in a training and consultancy role. Advisers usually work across a range of schools and often have specific areas of expertise.

Advisory Centre for Education (ACE) – An independent advice centre for parents, offering information about state education in England and Wales for 5 - 16 year olds. ACE offers free advice on topics such as exclusions, bullying, *special educational needs and school admission appeals. www.ace-ed.org.uk

Advisory teacher – An *LEA employee who performs a similar role to an adviser, but at a less senior level.

Affective learning – Learning which deals with emotions, feelings and beliefs.

Age Weighted Pupil Unit (AWPU) – The amount of money being spent on children in each *year group in the schools in a particular *LEA. The figure is weighted according to the number of children in each year group in the particular year of calculation.

Aggregated Schools' Budget (ASB) – Now called the *Individual Schools' Budget.

Agreed syllabus – A locally determined syllabus providing the legal basis for religious education in schools.

Aided school – *See *Voluntary Aided school.*

A-level – *See *Advanced-level.*

Annual parents' meeting – A meeting which the *governing body of a school must hold each year for parents/carers of children attending the institution. The purpose of the meeting is to give parents the opportunity to discuss what has happened at the school over the previous year and to outline the school's plans.

Annual report to parents – A written document which the *governing body of a school must issue to parents/carers of all children attending the institution. The report must be issued at least two weeks before the *annual parents' meeting. It must contain extensive details of the management and financial arrangements for the school and key examination/test statistics. Since May 2002 the report may be combined with the school *prospectus.

Annual review – A review of a child's *statement of special educational needs, carried out by the *LEA.

Annual schools' census – Now replaced by *Pupil Level Annual Schools' Census.

Appraisal – A system of professional development for teachers.

Approved Admission Number (AAN) – The maximum number of children that may be admitted to a school *year group in any one year.

AS-level – See *Advanced Subsidiary level.

Asperger's syndrome – A form of autism characterised by exceptional ability in one or more areas. People suffering from Asperger's syndrome can have difficulty communicating and forming relationships, but are often successful academically.

Assessment – A means of evaluating the performance and attainment of a child. *See also *formative assessment and *summative assessment.*

Assessment and Qualifications Alliance (AQA) – The largest of the three English examinations awarding bodies, offering a wide range of qualifications taken by over 750,000 students nationally. www.aqa.org.uk

Asset Management Plan (AMP) – An *LEA plan which aims to ensure the most efficient use of resources, distributed in a clearly transparent, unbiased and equitable manner. Such plans help schools continue to build on their strengths, in partnership with the LEA and other partner agencies.

Assistant head of department – A member of teaching staff who assists the *head of department in their management duties, and deputises for them in their absence.

Assistant head of faculty – A member of teaching staff who assists the *head of faculty in managing a faculty, and deputises for them in their absence. Assistant heads of faculty are sometimes also responsible for an individual department.

Assistant head of year – A member of teaching staff who assists the *head of year in organising *pastoral arrangements for a *year group, and who deputises for them in their absence.

Assistant headteacher – A senior member of staff in a *primary or *secondary school, two steps down from the headteacher. Assistant headteachers are usually in the *leadership group and take on key management responsibilities.

Assisted Places Scheme (APS) – A government scheme to fund places in independent schools for selected children.

Associate headteacher – A headteacher who works in an advisory role with a group of schools.

Association for Citizenship Teaching (ACT) – A membership organisation supporting teachers of citizenship. www.teachingcitizenship.org.uk

Association for Learning Technology (ALT) – A membership organisation which seeks to bring together all those with an interest in the use of learning technology. www.alt.ac.uk

Association for Science Education (ASE) – A membership organisation supporting teachers of science. www.ase.org.uk

Association for the Study of Primary Education – A national body committed to the advancement of primary education through collaborative study and action. www.aspe.org.uk

Association of Learning Providers (ALP) – A subscription organisation championing the work of learning providers throughout the UK. www.learningproviders.org.uk

Association of Teachers and Lecturers (ATL) – A professional association and trade union representing teachers, lecturers and education support staff. www.askatl.org.uk

Association of Teachers of Mathematics (ATM) – A membership organisation supporting teachers of mathematics. www.atm.org.uk

Asylum seeker children – Children whose parents are seeking political asylum in the UK.

Attainment – Achievement as measured by an individual's knowledge, skills and understanding in a particular area of learning.

Attainment level – Within the *National Curriculum, describes the types and range of performance that children working at that level should normally show. There are eight levels for each *attainment target, plus a description for exceptional performance above level 8.

Attainment Target (AT) – A target within the *National Curriculum which sets out the knowledge, skills and understanding which children of different abilities and maturities are expected to have by the end of each *key stage. Except for *citizenship, they consist of eight *attainment levels.

Attention Deficit Disorder (ADD) – See *Attention Deficit Hyperactivity Disorder*.

Attention Deficit Hyperactivity Disorder (ADHD) – A condition resulting in three main behaviour problems: hyperactivity, impulsive behaviour and a short attention span. It can sometimes occur without the hyperactivity, and is then known as *Attention Deficit Disorder (ADD).

Audio Visual Aids (AVA) – Aids used by the teacher to help with the teaching process.

Auditory learner – A learner who prefers to learn by hearing (sometimes called the auditory channel). See also *learning styles*.

Authentification – The process by which a teacher ensures that the work students submit for assessment in external examinations is their own.

Authorised absence – Absence which is given approval by the headteacher, for reasons which are considered legitimate. Children should be in school unless they are unwell or have a medical appointment, have special permission for special leave in extenuating circumstances, or are accompanying their parents/carers on a family holiday. *See also *unauthorised absence*.

Autism – A mental disability affecting an individual's capacity to form relationships, communicate, react to stimuli and interpret the world.

Autumn package – A document published annually by the *DfES containing national student performance data from key stage tests and formal examinations, and made available to schools and *LEAs. It is often used to judge a school's performance against all schools nationally or a group of similar schools.

Average Class Size (ACS) – The average number of children in a class within a school, *LEA or specified area.

Awarding body – An organisation that administers an external examination.

Bachelor of Education (BEd) – A four year *higher education qualification that permits an individual to teach in *primary or *secondary schools.

Banding – Grouping children according to ability, but not as narrowly as in *setting.

Baseline assessment – An *assessment carried out by a teacher which allows further progress to be determined. They are usually conducted by teachers when children begin *primary school and allow progress to be monitored. Since September 2002 such assessments have no longer been compulsory, and have been replaced by the *Foundation Stage Profile.

Basic Skills Agency (BSA) – The national development organisation for literacy and numeracy in England and Wales. The Basic Skills Agency is an independent charity funded mainly through donations from the *DfES and the Welsh Assembly government. www.basic-skills.co.uk

Beacon School – A school officially recognised by the *DfES as having key strengths which should be shared with neighbouring schools. Beacon Schools were given additional funding to enable them to work with nearby schools to promote good practice, but the funding was phased out in 2002. *See also *leading edge school.*

Behaviour management – The steps taken by a school or teacher to promote positive behaviour.

Behaviour Support Plan (BSP) – A plan drawn up by a school to help an individual child manage their behaviour so they can make good progress at school.

Benchmarking – The comparison of one school with another to determine the relative levels of success in examinations.

Best value – The legal obligation to obtain goods and services by the most effective, efficient and economic means available.

Bloom's taxonomy – Usually refers to a model which describes how children acquire knowledge.

Brain Gym® – Light physical activity designed to stimulate the brain and help learners sustain improved concentration.

Brainstorm(ing) – *See *thoughtshowering.*

British Educational Communications and Technology Agency (BECTA) – The government's lead agency for ICT in education. It supports the UK government and national organisations in the use and development of ICT in education to raise standards, widen access, improve skills and encourage effective management. www.becta.org.uk/index.cfm

British Educational Leadership, Management and Administration Society (BELMAS) – A society that seeks to advance the practice, teaching and study of educational management, administration and leadership in the UK, and to contribute to international developments in these areas. www.belmas.org.uk

Broadband – A fast internet connection which is up to ten times faster than conventional telephone lines. Broadband is becoming the standard means of schools connecting to the internet.

Budget – A financial representation of a *governing body's plan over a given period of time.

Budget plan – The spending intentions of a school *governing body for the financial year, drawn up with regard to the overall level of funding available to the school.

Budget share – A school's share of the *Individual Schools' Budget for any financial year, calculated using the *LEA's funding formula.

Burgundy book – A publication containing

the rules governing the national conditions of service for school teachers in *maintained schools in England and Wales.

Bursar – The member of staff responsible for running the day to day financial affairs of the school. The bursar is not normally a member of the teaching staff, but works closely with the headteacher. Also sometimes called the *school finance officer.

Bursar Development Programme (BDP) – A national programme to support the development of an effective market for bursars, developing both the supply and demand by providing suitable bursarial training. It is provided by the *National College for School Leadership.

Campaign for Learning – A national charity that aims to create an appetite for learning in individuals that will sustain them throughout their lives. It was created with the sole purpose of championing the cause of *lifelong learning.
www.campaign-for-learning.org.uk

Campaign for Real Education (CRE) – A campaign group which presses for higher standards and more parental choice in state education. www.cre.org.uk

Campaign for State Education (CASE) – An education campaign group which campaigns for the right of all to the highest quality state education, regardless of race, gender, home circumstances, ability or disability. www.casenet.org.uk

Capability – Defines a teacher's ability to teach at the required standard, even if he or she chooses not to do so.

Capital expenditure – Expenditure on major items such as land, new buildings and facilities, and under certain circumstances, repairs, maintenance and large items of equipment.

Capitation – The amount of money allocated for each subject area taught in a school. It is usually the responsibility of the *head of department or *subject co-ordinator to allocate this money effectively.

Career entry profile – A profile of the skills and experience of a teacher on entering the teaching profession.

Careers Service – The former name of *Connexions.

Cascading – A system used by those attending courses or training events for passing on information to other teaching colleagues. It involves the teacher who has attended the event sharing the main points with other staff.

Catchment area – The geographical area from which a school's student population is drawn.

Central services – Services provided to schools by the *LEA using funds which are centrally retained.

Certificate of achievement – A qualification for school leavers who would normally leave school without a formal qualification.

Child-centred education – Refers to teaching methods that put the emphasis on the child rather than the teacher. *Compare with *teacher-centred education.*

Circular – A statement issued by the *DfES to provide directives on government education policies.

Citizenship – A *National Curriculum subject concerned with people's place in society and the rights and responsibility this confers. It has been a compulsory subject in *secondary schools since September 2002, and is often taught as part of lessons in Personal, Social and Health Education.

Citizenship Foundation, The – An independent charity working to promote more effective citizenship through education about the law, democracy and society. www.citizenshipfoundation.org.uk

City academy – A flagship school set up in an inner city area to promote high educational standards.

City Learning Centres (CLC) – Education centres set up in *Excellence in Cities areas to promote specific aspects of learning with young people and the wider community.

Many CLCs are situated on school grounds or are attached to existing school buildings.

City Technology College (CTC) – Technology Colleges set up with assistance of private enterprise during the 1990s and receiving their funding directly from the *DfES.

Classroom organisation – The manner in which a teacher sets out their classroom and organises learning within it.

Classroom Support Assistant (CSA) – See *Teaching Assistant.

Closed question – A question only likely to lead to a yes or no answer.

Cloze – A technique used to develop literacy involving selected words being deleted from a text, and children being challenged to fill in the blanks.

Cluster – A group of local schools who share resources and or training events.

Code of Practice (COP) – Government guidance on managing specific aspects of school provision.

Cognitive – To do with the brain.

Cognitive Ability Test (CAT) – The score obtained from a standardised test in verbal reasoning, non-verbal reasoning and mathematical skills. The tests are usually given in year 7, and are seen as an indication of a child's potential.

Cognitive Acceleration through Mathematics Education (CAME) – A parallel scheme to *CASE but for mathematics education.

Cognitive Acceleration through Science Education (CASE) – A programme of lessons in science to promote effective learning. It focuses heavily on using *accelerated learning principles and developing *thinking skills. Studies have shown beneficial effects in science examinations for children undertaking CASE lessons, together with improvements in English and maths results.

Cognitive Acceleration through Technology Education (CATE) – A parallel scheme to *CASE but for technology education.

Cohort – A group of children, often referring to a *year group.

Collective worship – Schools are required to deliver a daily act of collective worship to all children, which normally takes place during registration.

College of Further Education (CFE) – A college offering *A-level and *vocational courses to young people and adults.

College of Higher Education (CHE) – A college offering degree level courses to young people and adults.

College of Teachers, The – A professional association for school teachers. www.collegeofteachers.ac.uk

Common Basic Data Set (CBDS) – A set of data definitions that provides a standard for data used in schools in their *Pupil Level Annual Schools' Census.

Common Pay Spine/Scale (CPS) – The pay levels set by the government for teachers in England.

Community education – Usually refers to education provided by a school to the wider community in addition to its students, often through evening classes.

Competence measures – A teacher is said to be subject to competence measures if they are being investigated due to concerns over their performance as a teacher.

Competitive tendering – The process of obtaining quotes from a variety of potential providers, before awarding contracts for goods or services.

Comprehensive school – A school which does not select children for admission on grounds of ability.

Compulsory Competitive Tendering (CCT) – The requirement for schools to obtain at least several quotes for maintenance or other work to be undertaken, to ensure *best value.

Compulsory school age – 5 - 16, the age during which children should normally be at school.

Conditions of employment – The rules setting out the conditions under which a teacher is employed. *See also *burgundy book.*

Connexions – The government's support service for all young people aged 13 - 19 in England. Previously called the Careers Service, it aims to provide integrated advice, guidance and access to personal development opportunities for this group and to help them make a smooth transition to adulthood and working life. www.connexions.gov.uk

Connexions card – The card issued to all young people in England to enable them to benefit from services offered by *Connexions.

Continuing Professional Development (CPD) – See *In-Service Education and Training.

Continuity – The concept of ensuring that one piece of work, or level of teaching, is maintained in a way that continues to challenge a child. Often used in the context of different key stages.

Continuous assessment – Judging children throughout the year rather than on a final examination.

Controlled school – See *Voluntary Controlled school.

Core curriculum – See *core subject.

Core subject – One of the three subjects (English, maths and science) in the *National Curriculum which are compulsory for all children of all ages.

Coursework – Work carried out during a course of study, and frequently used in *assessment.

Cover lesson – A lesson taken by a *supply teacher or a teacher who would not normally teach the class, in cases where the usual class teacher is absent. Also sometimes called an *invigilation.

Criterion referencing – A method of *assessment in which *attainment is judged according to specific levels or criteria, for example the *National Curriculum *attainment levels.

Cross-curricular – Involving several or all areas of the curriculum.

Cross-curricular theme – An aspect of the *National Curriculum which must be taught across all subjects.

Cultural diversity – Schools must make sure they design a curriculum which embraces the different cultures or ethnic groups of the school and the country as a whole.

Curriculum – The education offered to children in schools, as part of both the *National Curriculum and the so-called *hidden curriculum.

Curriculum Development Centre (CDC) – A support centre set up by an *LEA to facilitate curriculum development in schools. Such a centre usually has a bank of resources which may be borrowed by teachers.

Curriculum flexibility – The ability of schools to choose alternative curriculum arrangements for their children, if this is deemed appropriate.

Curriculum Online – The government's flagship programme to promote and make available digital learning materials for schools. *eLearning credits have been given to all schools to spend on such materials using information gained from a dedicated website. www.curriculumonline.gov.uk

Delegated budget – The budget share which is allocated to the school by the *LEA and is controlled by the school's *governing body.

Department for Education and Skills (DfES) – The government department responsible for providing education and skills development in England. www.dfes.gov.uk

Design and Technology Association – A professional organisation supporting teachers of design and technology in England. www.data.org.uk

Desirable outcomes – The knowledge, skills and understanding expected of children by the end of *reception year.

Detention – A punishment given to a child whereby they are kept under supervision after school, during the lunchtime or at break. Detentions are usually given for poor behaviour or failure to complete homework without a reasonable excuse. Schools must give parents/carers 24 hours notice of detention which will take place after school.

Development education – Education concerned with international development issues such as poverty, debt and human rights.

Development Education Centre (DEC) – A teacher resources centre providing curriculum materials to teach *development education.

Development manager/director – A member of staff in school carrying out the duties of *development officer, but at a more senior level in the school, often as part of the *senior management team.

Development officer – A member of staff in a school responsible for school fundraising. In the last few years there has been a large increase in the number of schools appointing development officers, as more schools try to access funds from external sources.

Development plan – See *School Improvement Plan*.

Devolved funds – Funds used by the school for specific purposes and within a fixed period of time.

DfES – See *Department for Education and Skills*.

Didactic teaching – A traditional method of teaching involving whole class instruction.

Differentiation – The process of effectively matching the needs of learners to the tasks given. For example, a teacher must ensure that appropriate levels of challenge are provided to all children, so that during a lesson no child finds tasks too difficult or too easy.

Directed Activity Related to Text (DART) – An activity such as *cloze, sequencing or prediction, which requires students to interact with text, so helping them to a better understanding.

Directed time – Time when teachers must be available to carry out their duties under the direction of the headteacher. A full-time teacher's directed time amounts to 1,265 hours in any school year. Marking, preparation and administration fall outside directed time.

Disability Discrimination Act (DDA) – A law designed to ensure equality of opportunity and access for people with disabilities.

Disapplication – A term used where *National Curriculum requirements may not apply to an individual child.

Distance learning – Learning carried out remotely from the teacher or tutor; for example using online resources.

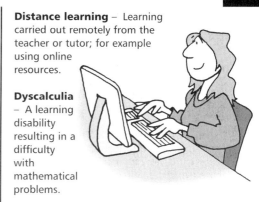

Dyscalculia – A learning disability resulting in a difficulty with mathematical problems.

Dyslexia – A condition which results in difficulty with reading and writing. Some educationalists prefer the term *specific learning difficulty.

Dyspraxia – A condition which results in restricted motor movement.

Early years – Used mainly to refer to children who are between 5 and 7 years old.

Earmarked funds – Funds which have been allocated to the school separately from the *budget share and which must be used for a particular purpose.

EDEXCEL – One of the largest examining and awarding bodies in the UK. www.edexcel.org.uk

Education Action Zone (EAZ) – Clusters of schools in inner cities which receive extra funds to tackle agreed priorities, under the guidance of the *LEA. Many EAZs were set up to address underachievement and poor attendance in socially deprived areas.

Educational Psychologist (Ed. Psych.; EP) – An *LEA employee whose role is to make assessments about the education of individual children and recommend actions to help them make progress at school. They work mainly with children with social and/or behavioural difficulties.

Educational Visits Co-ordinator (EVC) – All schools are now required to assign the role of EVC to a senior teacher.

Education Business Partnership (EBP) – An organisation providing support to schools in developing business and enterprise links.

Educational Development Plan (EDP) – A plan published by an *LEA setting out priorities for education over a number of years.

Education Extra – The leading charity that supports *out-of-school-hours learning

in schools. Merged in October 2003 with CEDC to form ContinYou.

Education for Sustainable Development (ESD) – A *cross-curricular theme within the *National Curriculum, focusing on environmental education and the need to manage the earth's resources.

Education Maintenance Allowance (EMA) – A government pilot scheme providing up to £40 a week for young people during term time if they stay in full-time education and training.

Education Other Than At School (EOTAS) – Refers to children being educated at home. *See *parental home education.*

Education Otherwise (EO) – *See *Education Other Than At School.*

Education Supervision Order (ESO) – A court order imposed on a child who it is felt is not being educated properly. The order, which lasts for one year initially, allows an *LEA supervisor to work in partnership with the child and his/her family to ensure he/she receives an appropriate education.

Education Welfare Officer (EWO) – An *LEA employee who works with individual children to help them attend school regularly.

Education Welfare Service (EWS) – A division within an LEA dealing with school attendance issues.

eLearning – Learning through electronic media, particularly the internet.

eLearning Credit (ELC) – A government grant given directly to schools to purchase digital learning materials from *Curriculum Online. The first eLearning Credits were given out in 2002-2003.

Eleven Plus – An examination, taken in the last year of primary school, which determines whether a child can attend a *grammar school. The eleven plus used to be taken nationally when grammar schools were widespread, but is now confined to the few *LEAs that retain their grammar schools.

Emotional and Behavioural Difficulty/Disorder (EBD) – Any difficulty linked to emotions or behaviour that presents a barrier to learning.

English as an Additional Language (EAL) – Refers to children whose first language is not English. Such children often receive additional help to overcome this potential barrier to learning through specialist *teaching assistants. Used to be called English as a second language.

English Association, The – A membership organisation which aims to further

But, soft! What light

knowledge, understanding and enjoyment of the English language and literature, and to foster good practice in its teaching and learning at all levels. www.le.ac.uk/engassoc

Enquiry – Usually refers to a type of learning involving students posing questions, and seeking the information to answer them. It is especially popular in science and geography.

Enrichment – Usually refers to the provision of extra activities *out-of-school hours that enhance the *core curriculum.

Entitlement – Refers to the right of every child, regardless of race, gender, social background or disability, to a certain level of education and development under the *National Curriculum.

Ethnic monitoring – The monitoring of attainment of minority ethnic children to minimise the risk of underachievement.

European Computer Driving Licence (ECDL) – The European-wide qualification which enables people to demonstrate their competence in computer skills. www.ecdl.co.uk

Examinations Appeals Board (EAB) – An independent body, set up by government in 1999, to help give confidence, to those who make use of the examinations system, that the grades awarded are fair and accurate. The Board hears appeals on a range of examinations and is the final stage of the enquiries and appeals process after the awarding body responsible for the examination has done its work. Private candidates and examination centres may pursue enquiries about individual results, but students must approach their school to enquire on their behalf. www.theeab.org.uk

Excellence Challenge – A government initiative, begun in 2001, to address the under-representation of students from disadvantaged backgrounds in post-16 and higher education.

Excellence clusters – A government attempt to bring the benefits of *Excellence in Cities to small pockets of deprivation. Groups of schools work in partnership to focus on the needs and aspirations of individual students and their parents, supported by additional government funding.

Excellence in Cities (EiC) – A government initiative to improve education in the inner cities. Extra income is provided to schools and *LEA-wide action plans set targets for improvement.

Exclusion – The removal of a child from school, usually due to serious breaches of discipline or misconduct. There are *fixed-term and *permanent exclusions.

Exclusion appeal – A hearing to which parents/carers have the right to refer a school's decision to exclude their child from school.

Exemplar – Usually refers to an example of a child's work at a particular level to help others understand what is required to reach that level.

Experiential learning – Learning through concrete experiences.

Extension tasks – Tasks carried out by children who have completed work early or require particularly challenging activities because they are *more able.

External assessment – Assessment, such as a *GCSE or *A-level, carried out by an external body.

Extra-curricular – Outside the main *curriculum. Usually refers to lunchtime and after school activities which support and supplement elements of the *National Curriculum.

Fair funding – A system, introduced in 1999, that allows schools to develop further their capacity for self-government by being more directly responsible for funding arrangements themselves. It is used by *LEAs to calculate the budgets of all schools maintained by them, and sets the framework for the financial relationship that operates between schools and their LEAs.

Fast track teaching – A government scheme for existing and trainee teachers with the potential to become leaders in education. It provides an enhanced support and career development structure. Fast track teachers get paid more and have the chance to work in a wide variety of schools.

Feeder school – The *primary schools that children in a *secondary school have come from are known as its feeder schools.

Financial year – The 12-month period from 1 April to 31 March. The budgets of all schools run in financial years.

Fine motor skills – Skills, such as holding a pen correctly or moving the lips to eat food, which require the fine manipulation of hands, feet or other parts of the body.

First school – A *primary school which takes children from age 5 to age 8/9, when they transfer to a *middle school.

Fixed-term exclusion – Where a child is excluded from school for a limited period of time. This can last from one to 45 days, and a definite return date to school must be given. No child can be excluded from school for more than 45 days in one academic year.

Form 7 – *See *Pupil Level Annual Schools' Census.*

Formative assessment – Assessment that provides feedback to improve teaching and learning, rather than for grading or putting in rank order. *Compare with *summative assessment.*

Form tutor – A teacher, usually in a *secondary school, who has responsibility for taking the daily attendance register for their *tutor group. Form tutors also help with the *pastoral care of the children in their class, and may also teach them Personal, Health and Social Education.

SALLY

Formula funding – The method by which funds for school budgets are calculated by *LEAs. The main factor affecting the amount of funding delegated to schools is the number of children on roll.

Foundation stage – A curriculum for children of nursery and reception age. Part of the statutory *National Curriculum for England.

Foundation Stage Profile (FSP) – The new name for *baseline assessment.

Foundation subject – Any subject which at some stage must be taught as a compulsory part of the *National Curriculum. The *core subjects of English, mathematics and science are also strictly speaking foundation subjects, and the term 'non-core foundation subjects' is often used to identify foundation subjects other than English, mathematics and science. *See also page 64.*

Foundation tier – *See *tier.*

Four-part lesson structure – The recommended structure for the *National Literacy Strategy, comprising *starter, introduction, development and *plenary.

Fresh Start school – A new maintained school which is designed to replace a closing school (or schools) requiring *special measures. Schools with *serious weaknesses, those subject to a formal warning or those achieving less than a 15% rate for five GCSEs at A*-C fall into this category. Government approval is necessary for acceptance into the Fresh Start programme.

Further Education (FE) – Education after the statutory school age but normally below degree level. It usually takes place in colleges of further education.

Gap year – A year during which students take a break from education, usually between taking their A-levels and beginning their university courses. Many young people undertake voluntary work, or go travelling during their gap year.

General Certificate of Education (GCE) – The category of qualification into which *AS- and *A-levels fall.

General Certificate of Secondary Education (GCSE) – The examination taken by most children in year 11 (age 15-16) at the end of their compulsory education. GCSEs are split into different *tiers which allow students to access specific grade bands.

General National Vocational Qualification (GNVQ) – A vocational qualification, an alternative to *GCSE, taken at age 16, now being replaced by *vocational GCSEs.

General Teaching Council (GTC) – The professional body regulating the work of teachers. Membership is compulsory for all teachers working in schools in England. www.gtce.org.uk

Geographical Association, The – The professional association for teachers of geography in schools.
www.geography.org.uk

Gifted – A gifted child is defined by the *DfES as a child who achieves, or has the ability to achieve, significantly above their peers in their school. Gifted children are very able in one or more of the *National Curriculum *core subjects, or are 'all-rounders'. Extra funding has been provided through *Excellence in Cities to enhance provision for these children and schools are required to identify the top 5-10% of children in each year group to benefit from the new initiatives.

Gifted and Talented Co-ordinator – A member of staff responsible for organising provision for more able children in a school or *LEA. See also *gifted and *talented.

Governing body – The body with legal responsibility for the running of the school, comprising a group of *governors.

Governor – An unpaid individual who assists the headteacher in the running of the school as part of a *governing body.

Graduate teacher training programme An employment-based training programme leading to the award of *Qualified Teacher Status, aimed particularly at graduates with experience in other professional fields.

Grammar school – A school taking only children of higher ability, usually determined by a test taken at age 11. A few *LEAs in England still retain grammar schools.

Grammar school ballot – A vote which determines whether a *grammar school's selective status should be abolished.

Parents/carers of existing and prospective students may be entitled to vote in such ballots.

Grant-Maintained School (GMS) – A *maintained school that voluntarily withdrew itself from local authority support, and instead was maintained directly by central government. The scheme was abolished in the late 1990s.

Graphicacy – The ability to understand and represent spatial information using visual means such as graphs and charts.

Gross motor skills – Skills involving larger movements of the limbs and body, such as running and jumping. *Compare with *fine motor skills*.

Guided reading – A method of supporting children's independent reading skills through teacher intervention. Small groups of children of similar reading ability read a text introduced by the teacher, who uses a range of strategies to encourage critical understanding and thoughtful reflection.

Head of Department (HOD) – A member of staff responsible for a particular subject area, usually in a *secondary school. Their duties include planning the curriculum in their subject area, overseeing the work of staff and managing the departmental budget. May also be called a *subject leader.

Head of Faculty (HOF) – A member of staff in a secondary school responsible for managing a broad aspect of the curriculum, eg: humanities, science.

Head of Year (HOY) – A member of staff responsible for the *pastoral care of a particular *year group, usually in a *secondary school.

Headteacher Induction Programme (HIP) – A programme to support newly appointed headteachers in their first headship, organised by the *National College of School Leadership.

Headteachers' Leadership And Management Programme (HEADLAMP) A programme of professional development for headteachers, which is being replaced by the Headteacher Induction Programme.

Her Majesty's Inspector of Schools (HMI) – Government education specialists, employed by *OFSTED, who monitor the progress of schools judged to have *serious weaknesses and monitor and carry out repeat inspections for those in *special measures. They do not normally get involved in standard school inspections.

Hidden curriculum – Usually refers to the informal, incidental learning that takes place as a result of students being part of a school community. This includes learning about relationships, social skills and values.

Higher Education (HE) – Education within universities, or colleges offering degree courses.

Higher Level Teaching Assistant (HLTA) – A *teaching assistant who has undergone additional training to work in a more senior capacity.

Higher order thinking skills – Thinking skills, such as evaluation, which require sustained effort for most students to achieve.

Higher tier – See *tier.

Historical Association, The – The professional body supporting the teaching of history in schools. www.history.org.uk

Home education – See *parental home education*.

Home-School Agreement (HSA) – An agreement drawn up between a school and a parent/carer which aims to create a sense of partnership.

Humanities Association – The professional body supporting the teaching of humanities in schools. www.hums.org.uk

In-class support – Support for individual students provided in the classroom by *teaching assistants.

Inclusion – The process through which a school seeks to recognise and encourage each individual, enabling them to access, the curriculum and to participate and achieve fully.

Independent school – A school which receives its funding from sources outside the *DfES. Sometimes also called a *private school.

Independent/state school partnership A government-supported partnership between an *independent and a *state school, designed to promote the sharing of good practice and resources.

Individual Behaviour Plan (IBP) – A document setting out behaviour targets for an individual student and how a school will provide support to help the student reach them. Individual Behaviour Plans are usually drawn up by a school in consultation with the student and their parents/carers.

Individual Education Plan (IEP) – A planning document which describes a child's *special educational needs and the arrangements a school is making to meet these.

Individual Schools' Budget (ISB) – The balance of the *Local Schools' Budget after the centrally retained funds have been deducted. The ISB (known previously as the Aggregated Schools' Budget) is given out to schools according to the *funding formula.

Induction – Usually refers to the process of supporting a new teacher during their first year at a school. Also used to refer to the support provided to a member of staff who is promoted to a new post.

Induction day – A day during which children in year 6 get to visit, during a working day, the secondary school they will attend from year 7 onwards. It normally takes place late in the summer term of the school year before entry and allows the child to meet some of their new teachers and become acquainted with their new school.

Infant – A child between 5 and 7 years of age. *See also *early years.*

Infant school – A school providing education for children age 5 - 7. *See also *junior school.*

In loco parentis – A legal term meaning in place of the parent. A teacher and school must show the same duty of care towards a child as would a reasonable parent.

In-Service Education and Training (INSET) – Training carried out to improve the professional competence of teachers.

INSET takes place in school on pre-arranged days when students are not present, or on external courses, but usually in term time.

Inspection – *See *Office for Standards in Education*.

Integration – The education of children with *special educational needs in *mainstream schools.

Intelligence quotient (IQ) – The traditional way of measuring intelligence, now considered by many educationalists to be out of date. IQ has been replaced by the theory of *multiple intelligences.

Intermediate tier – *See *tier*.

International Baccalaureate (IB) – A post-16 qualification taken in some schools in England in preference to A-levels. The IB is broader in its scope than *A-levels, and is thought by some to result in a more rounded qualification than that offered by the *A-levels. www.ibo.org

Intranet – A computer environment that simulates access to the internet by holding large numbers of pages on in internal server. Many schools in England have intranet connections in addition to their external connections to the internet.

Invigilation (invigilator) – Teachers or other school staff being present to oversee students taking public examinations, or to take a *cover lesson.

ISDN – A fast internet connection used in some schools, but not as fast as *broadband.

Junior school – A school providing education for children age 8 - 11. *See also *infant school*.

Key skills – Essential skills that underpin success in education, employment, lifelong learning and personal development. They cover:
- Communication
- Application of number
- Information technology
- Working with others
- Improving own learning and performance
- Problem-solving

Key Stages (1-4) – Periods of two to three years children spend on each part of the *National Curriculum, beginning in Key Stage 1 at age 5 - 7 and ending in Key Stage 4, age 14 - 16.

Age	Stage	Year
3-4	Foundation	
4-5	Foundation	Reception
5-6	Key Stage 1	Year 1
6-7	Key Stage 1	Year 2
7-8	Key Stage 2	Year 3
8-9	Key Stage 2	Year 4
9-10	Key Stage 2	Year 5
10-11	Key Stage 2	Year 6
11-12	Key Stage 3	Year 7
12-13	Key Stage 3	Year 8
13-14	Key Stage 3	Year 9
14-15	Key Stage 4	Year 10
15-16	Key Stage 4	Year 11

Key Stage 3 consultant – An *LEA *advisory teacher who supports schools in the implementation of the *Key Stage 3 Strategy.

Key Stage 3 National Strategy (Key Stage 3 Strategy) – A government initiative to improve teaching and learning for 11 - 14 year olds.

Kinaesthetic learner – A learner who prefers to learn by doing (sometimes called the kinaesthetic channel). *See also *learning styles.*

Language support teacher – *See *Teaching Assistant.*

Laptops for teachers – A government scheme to improve access to ICT for teachers, by providing free or subsidised machines.

Leadership group – The most senior management team in a school, usually comprising the headteacher, deputy headteacher(s) and assistant headteacher(s).

Leadership incentive grant – A government grant scheme which is intended to ensure that leadership teams in schools are able to transform the delivery of education. The focus is on collaboration between schools in order to strengthen leadership, enhance the quality of teaching and learning and establish a culture of high expectations.

Leadership Programme for Service Headteachers (LPSH) – A programme of professional development for headteachers provided by the *National College of School Leadership.

Leading edge school – A school receiving additional funding from the government to develop innovative approaches to education provision. Successful schools are likely already to be known as innovators in their field.

Leading from the middle – A new professional development programme for school *middle managers, organised by the *National College for School Leadership.

League table – A government analysis of school assessment and examination results in rank order. *See also *performance table.*

Learndirect – A network of online learning and information services, sponsored by the government, to explore flexible learning. The aim is to create a learning society where everyone can learn and upgrade their skills throughout life. www.learndirect.co.uk

Learning and Skills Council (LSC) – The body responsible for funding and planning education and training for young people over 16 years old in England. www.lsc.gov.uk

Learning journal – A diary documenting what has been learned by a student during a period of study.

Learning mentor – A member of staff responsible for helping individual children make academic progress, usually within a *Learning Support Unit.

Learning objective – What a teacher intends their students to gain from a lesson or part of a lesson. *See also *learning outcome.*

Learning outcome – The knowledge, skills and understanding that children gain from a lesson, sequence of lessons or *scheme of work. Teachers are required to include learning outcomes in their *lesson plans, and are increasingly encouraged to share these with children at the start of the lesson.

Learning partnership – A non-statutory, voluntary grouping of local learning providers, ranging from the voluntary sector to higher education institutes, which intend to create greater coherence in post-16 learning provision.

Learning Resource Centre (LRC) – A modern name for the school library.

Learning style – The particular method of learning preferred by a child. In recent years there has been a general acceptance that learning styles fall into three categories:
• Auditory – through hearing
• Kinaesthetic – though doing
• Visual – through seeing

As part of the *accelerated learning approach teachers are now encouraged to vary their *teaching styles to include all three types of learners.

Learning Support Assistant (LSA) – See *Teaching Assistant.

Learning Support Unit (LSU) – Usually refers to a room within a school dedicated to supporting individual children, often those who are disaffected or who find it difficult to work in classrooms. They are staffed by *learning mentors.

Learning Through Landscapes (LTL) – A charity working to improve the environmental quality and educational use of school grounds. www.ltl.org.uk

Less able – A child is described as less able if they have lower than average ability for their age.

Lesson observation – A developmental process which involves a teacher observing a colleague teach in order to help either or both (but usually the observed) to improve the quality of their teaching.

Lesson plan – A written summary of an intended lesson, including details of the *learning outcomes, *resources to be used, tasks to be set and homework to be issued.

Level – See *attainment level.

Level description – Within the *National Curriculum refers to the types and range of performance which need to be demonstrated for the award of a specific level within the *attainment target. Level descriptions also apply to specific grades within GCSEs.

Licensed teacher – A person who is not a qualified teacher, but has been granted a licence to teach by the government.

Lifelong learning – The concept of learning extending from childhood, through working life and into retirement.

Literacy – Reading and writing skills.

Literacy Strategy – See *National Literacy Strategy*.

Local Education Authority (LEA) – The branch of local government responsible for ensuring schools meet their statutory duty to educate children at the local level.

Local Management of Schools (LMS) – A government initiative to improve the provision of education by making schools more responsive to the needs of their students and community, and enabling them to plan their use of resources to maximum effect in accordance with their needs and priorities. It has resulted in schools being more accountable for their finances.

Local Schools' Budget (LSB) – The total of all direct and indirect expenditure of an *LEA's schools.

London Challenge – An initiative launched in 2002 to transform the standards of secondary education in London. A key element is additional funding for training, especially addressing leadership issues in schools.

Looked-after children – Children who do not live with their parents. Most looked-after children live with foster parents, in children's homes or residential schools.

Lower school – Usually refers to the part of a secondary school catering for students in years 7 - 9.

Mainstream school – An ordinary, rather than a *special school.

Maintained school – Any school funded by the government via an *LEA scheme for financing schools. Nursery schools and *Pupil Referral Units, which have separate funding arrangements, are not included.

Management allowance – A salary enhancement provided to a member of staff in a school for a specific additional role, e.g. *subject leader.

Mark scheme – A written document which explains how teachers should award marks for a particular piece of work or examination.

Mathematical Association, The – A professional body supporting the teaching of mathematics in schools. www.m-a.org.uk

Mentor – A person who helps individual children make academic progress through one-to-one support or counselling sessions. *See also *learning mentor and *peer mentor.*

Metacognition – Understanding of how you think and reason. Sometimes referred to as 'thinking about thinking'.

Middle manager – A member of staff with key management duties within a school, such as a *head of department.

Middle school – A school providing education for children usually age 8 - 13, or occasionally 14. Depending on whether the majority of children are under or over the age of 11, middle schools are legally designated as either primary or secondary.

Middle Years Information System (Mid-Yis) – An information system which provides a baseline for *value added assessments in secondary schools. The Mid-Yis tests are designed to be taken on entry to the secondary school by students in years 7 - 9, and provide predictions of key stage 3 and GCSE performance.

Mind Map® – A visual representation of a topic or concept, with the key ideas radiating out from the centre, like the roots of a tree. Mind Maps® were developed by Tony Buzan and are an example of an *accelerated learning technique.

Minority ethnic group – Refers to students who, although born in the UK, have a different ethnic heritage, e.g. Asian or African-Caribbean. Many of these students have a heritage linked with British Commonwealth countries.

Mixed-ability teaching – The teaching of children of all abilities together, rather than in a *set or *stream.

Modelling – The process whereby a teacher demonstrates how they perform a task themselves in order to help students see how it can be done effectively.

Moderate Learning Difficulties (MLD) – Learning difficulties that do not usually have a pronounced effect on academic progress.

Moderation – A process whereby different teachers mark the same piece of work to agree a standard.

Modern languages assistant – Usually refers to an individual who works in small groups with students who are learning a modern foreign language. Modern languages assistants are usually students learning English at an overseas university.

Modular syllabus – An examination syllabus made up of several separate elements that can be assessed at different points throughout the year.

Module – A discrete unit of work within a course.

Monitoring – Following progress to determine success.

More able – Refers to a child who is of above average ability for their age. See also *gifted.

Multicultural education – Education that encourages children to recognise the contribution different cultures and ethnic groups make to the world.

Multiple intelligences – The theory of intelligence that maintains that people are intelligent in many ways, not just in terms of their *Intelligence Quotient. Put forward by Harvard Professor Howard Gardner in the 1980s, the theory suggests that people are intelligent in at least the following ways:

• Interpersonal
• Intrapersonal
• Linguistic

- Kinaesthetic
- Mathematical/logical
- Musical
- Natural
- Visual-Spatial

It has been embraced by many educational professionals and is a popular element of *accelerated learning programmes.

Music Masters' and Mistresses' Association – A membership organisation supporting the teaching of music in schools. www.mma-online.org.uk

National Academy for Gifted and Talented Youth (NAGTY) – England's national academy for more able children, based at Warwick University. The academy offers training courses for teachers as well as summer schools and other educational opportunities for very able children. www.warwick.ac.uk/gifted

National Association for Able Children in Education (NACE) – A charity supporting the needs of very able children. www.nace.co.uk

National Association for Gifted Children (NAGC) – A charity supporting the needs of very able children. www.nagcbritain.org.uk

National Association for Primary Education (NAPE) – A membership organisation promoting high quality primary education for every child. www.rmplc.co.uk/orgs/nape

National Association for Special Educational Needs (NASEN) – The leading organisation working to promote the education and development of all those with *special educational needs. www.nasen.org.uk

National Association for the Teaching of English (NATE) – A membership organisation supporting the teaching of English in schools. www.nate.org.uk

National Association of Head Teachers (NAHT) – The principal trade union representing headteachers in England. www.naht.org.uk

National Association of Music Educators (NAME) – A membership organisation supporting the teaching of music in schools.

National Association of Schoolmasters Union of Women Teachers (NASUWT) – One of the largest teachers' unions. www.teachersunion.org.uk

National Bursars Association (NBA) – The leading professional association for bursars working in schools. www.nba.org.uk

National College for School Leadership (NCSL) – An organisation set up by the government to provide career-long learning and development opportunities and support for existing and aspiring teachers in England. www.ncsl.org.uk

National Curriculum (NC) – The compulsory curriculum for all children in state schools in England, as set out by the *DfES. The statutory subjects are shown overleaf. www.nc.uk.net

	Key stage 1	Key stage 2	Key stage 3	Key stage 4	Core subjects	Non-core foundation subjects
Age	5-7	7-11	11-14	14-16		
Year groups	1-2	3-6	7-9	10-11		
English	•	•	•	•	•	
Mathematics	•	•	•	•	•	
Science	•	•	•	•	•	
Design & technology	•	•	•	•		•
ICT	•	•	•	•		•
History	•	•	•			•
Geography	•	•	•			•
Modern foreign languages			•	•		•
Art & design	•	•	•			•
Music	•	•	•			•
Physical education	•	•	•	•		•
Citizenship			•	•		•

Based on The National Curriculum (1999)

National Curriculum level – *See *attainment level.*

National Foundation for Educational Research (NFER) – The UK's leading independent research organisation carrying out research in the field of education and training. www.nfer.ac.uk

National Grid for Learning (NGfL) – The main government educational portal site on the internet, with contributions from schools, museums, cultural bodies and industry. www.ngfl.gov.uk

National learning targets – National educational targets set by the government for young people and adults.

National Literacy Strategy (NLS) – A government initiative to support teachers working to improve *literacy in *primary schools.

National Numeracy Strategy (NNS) – A government initiative to support teachers working to improve *numeracy in *primary schools.

National Playing Fields Association (NPFA) – An organisation dedicated to protecting and improving playing fields and playgrounds. www.npfa.co.uk

National Professional Qualification for Headship (NPQH) – A development programme to prepare candidates for the role of headship, organised by the *National College for School Leadership.

National Society for Education in Art and Design – A membership organisation concerned with art, craft and design teaching across all phases of education. www.nsead.org.

National standards for headteachers – Standards published by the *DfES setting out the knowledge, understanding, skills and attributes which relate to the key areas of headship.

National standards for subject leaders – A document, published by the *DfES, setting out the skills required by effective subject leaders. It is used to help identify professional development needs.

National Union of Teachers (NUT) – A principal professional association for teachers. www.teachers.org.uk

Newly Qualified Teacher (NQT) – A teacher in their first year of teaching after gaining *Qualified Teacher Status. NQTs usually have a reduced timetable and receive *induction to help them settle into their new post.

Non-contact time – Time during the school day when a teacher is not teaching.

Non-statutory guidance – Guidance provided by the *DfES on educational issues which cannot be legally enforced.

Non-Teaching Assistant (NTA) – See *Teaching Assistant.

Norm-referenced assessment – An assessment in which a group of students is assessed, their marks placed in rank order and grades awarded to divisions of that order.

Number On/Of Roll (NOR) – The total number of students currently enrolled at a school.

Numeracy – Ability in the principles of mathematics.

Numeracy strategy – See *National Numeracy Strategy

Office for Standards in Education (OFSTED) – A non-ministerial government department, independent of the *DfES, whose remit is to improve standards of achievement and quality of education through regular independent inspection, public reporting and independent advice. www.ofsted.gov.uk

Open-ended question – A question that is likely to result in a thoughtful, in-depth answer. Open-ended questions are being promoted as a way to help develop *higher-order thinking skills. *Compare with *closed question.*

Oracy – Speaking skills.

Out-of-school hours – Refers to time when students are at school but are not engaged in lessons, registration or assembly. It includes lunch and breaktimes.

Outturn statement – A statement of what a school actually spent during a full *financial year.

Oxford Cambridge and RSA Examinations (OCR) – One of the three major examining bodies in England. www.ocr.org.uk

Parental Contribution (PC) – Usually refers to a school's request for a financial contribution from parents/carers towards the cost of an educational visit.

Parental home education – A situation where a parent/carer keeps their child at home to be educated rather than sending them to school. This is perfectly legal providing they can prove that a minimum standard of education is being met.

Parental preference – The legal right of parents to express a preference for the school they would like their child to attend.

Parent governor – A parent elected to the governing body to represent the interests of parents.

Parent Partnership Scheme (PPS) – An *LEA scheme to work more closely with parents/carers, especially those who have children with *special educational needs.

Parent-Teacher Association (PTA) – An informal group of parents/carers and teachers which supports the school, for example by organising fundraising activities, or helping out on open evenings.

Partnership teaching – *See *team teaching.*

Passive learning – Learning with minimal student contribution. *See also *active learning.*

Pastoral – Refers to the personal and social welfare of children whilst they are at school. Schools are required to write pastoral care policies which outline the measures they will take to ensure these areas are catered for.

Pastoral support plan – A school-based intervention to help individual children manage their behaviour.

Pathfinder school – A school participating in a government pilot to explore ways of improving the effectiveness and efficiency of the school workforce. The package to participating schools includes laptops for every teacher, additional support staff, and extra training and support to enable teachers to have more *non-contact time.

Pay spine – A nationally applicable listing of the rates of pay to which teachers are entitled, according to their experience and qualifications.

Pedagogy – The methods used to teach and the way the curriculum is put together.

Peer mentor – A child who acts as a *mentor to another child.

Performance and Assessment Data report (PANDA) – A detailed report sent to all schools by the *DfES each year as part of the *autumn package of pupil performance information. It contains essential data on attainment and attendance and compares a school with others of a similar background. The PANDA report is sent to schools to aid self-evaluation and the development of plans to raise standards.

Performance Indicators for Value Added Target Setting (PIVATS) – An assessment management tool for children with learning difficulties performing within the *p-levels, or at levels 1-4 where these are significantly below national expectations for children of similar age.

Performance Indicators in Primary Schools (PIPS) – An information system which monitors attainment, *value added and attitudes in primary age children.

Performance management – The main *appraisal system for teachers.

Performance table – Information on school performance in each *LEA, with local and national averages. *See also *league table.*

Peripatetic – Refers to a teacher who travels to several schools in the course of their work, often spending only a few hours in each a week. There are many peripatetic teachers who teach instrumental music.

Permanent exclusion – An *indefinite exclusion which results in a child having to be placed in an alternative school or, in some cases, in a *Pupil Referral Unit.

Physical Education Association of the United Kingdom – A membership association which exists to promote, develop and sustain high quality physical education in schools.
www.pea.uk.com

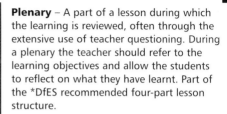

Plenary – A part of a lesson during which the learning is reviewed, often through the extensive use of teacher questioning. During a plenary the teacher should refer to the learning objectives and allow the students to reflect on what they have learnt. Part of the *DfES recommended four-part lesson structure.

P-levels/scales – Performance levels for children who do not reach *National Curriculum level 1. They were designed to help identify children with *special educational needs.

Policy – A written document outlining a school's position on a key area of its practice.

Post-16 – Refers to children in years 12 and 13 at schools and colleges.

Postgraduate Certificate of Education (PGCE) – The certificate awarded to individuals who have completed a one year university teacher training course, which must be preceded by a first degree.

Post-OFSTED action plan – A written plan prepared by the *governing body within 40 days of an *OFSTED inspection in response to key issues identified in the inspection report. The plan is a public document and is usually sent to all parents/carers with children at the school.

Pre-Inspection Commentary (PIC) – A document written by a registered *OFSTED inspector prior to a school inspection, outlining the context for a forthcoming school inspection.

Primary school – A school providing education to children age 5 - 11. *See also *infant school and *junior school.*

Private Finance Initiative (PFI) – A government scheme which aims to provide better, more cost-effective public services through partnership with the private sector. Under the scheme private companies build and maintain schools which are leased back to the *LEA.

Probationary teacher – *See *Newly Qualified Teacher.*

Professional Association of Teachers (PAT) – An independent trade union and professional association for teachers. www.pat.org.uk

Professional development – *See *In-Service Education and Training*.

Profiling – The recording of children's personal achievements in areas of activity other than examination performance.

Profound and Multiple Learning Difficulties (PMLD) – Refers to students who are likely to have more than one severe disability.

Programme of Study (POS) – Within the *National Curriculum, the knowledge, skills and processes which are required to be taught to students during each *key stage.

Progress file – A set of materials designed to support the processes of planning, achieving and reviewing for individual students. It will replace the *Record of Achievement.

Progression – Ensuring that children make progress in line with their previous achievements.

Prospectus – A written document setting out key information about a school, including admission arrangements, curriculum provision and extra-curricular activities. It is used by prospective parents/carers to help them judge whether the school is appropriate for their child.

Psychology and Assessment Service (PAS) – An *LEA service supporting children with learning or behavioural difficulties. The service is usually staffed by educational psychologists who make assessments of children's *special educational needs.

Published Admissions Limit (PAL) – The maximum number of students a school can admit to a *year group in any one year.

Pupil-centred learning – See *student-centred learning.*

Pupil Level Annual Schools' Census (PLASC) – A data collection exercise carried out by all schools in England

on behalf of the *DfES on school census day – usually in January.

Pupil Referral Unit (PRU) – An educational establishment maintained by an LEA providing education to students who have been excluded from schools.

Pupil/Teacher Ratio (PTR) – The number of students per teacher in a school or class.

Pyramid – A group of schools comprising a *secondary school and its *feeder *middle and/or *primary schools. The pyramid of schools meets to make plans for collaborative working.

assessments, and to accredit and monitor qualifications in schools, colleges and at work. www.qca.org.uk

Qualified Teacher Status (QTS) – A certificate awarded to an individual that enables them to teach in schools in England.

Qualitative – Relating to quality. Used mainly in the context of more subjective information gained on students' performance by teachers which does not easily translate into numerical information or statistical data.

QTS skills – The skills that must be acquired by an individual before they are awarded *Qualified Teacher Status.

Qualifications and Curriculum Authority (QCA) – A government agency that works to maintain and develop the school curriculum and associated

Quantitative – Relating to quantity. Used mainly to refer to information on students gained from hard data such as tests and examinations which easily translates into numerical information or statistical data.

Quorum – The minimum number of people required to be present at a meeting of a *governing body or committee in order that decisions can be taken.

Record of Achievement (ROA, REACH) – A document which children take with them when they leave formal education which outlines all their academic and non-academic achievements.

Re-engagement – Usually used to describe the process whereby children become motivated again in school work and take an interest in their learning.

Reflective journal – A diary, typically kept by a trainee teacher, that records teaching methods attempted and the results gained. The journal forms part of the assessment for *Qualified Teacher Status.

Refugee children – Children whose parents have been granted political asylum in this country.

Race equality – The concept of ensuring fair treatment for all, irrespective of their race or ethnic origin.

Reception – The first class of a *primary school, taking mostly children who are 5 years old.

Registered Inspector (RgI/RI) – An official qualified to carry out and lead a school *OFSTED inspection.

Registration – The time, at the beginning of both morning and afternoon school, during which a teacher marks the attendance register for the children in their *tutor group.

Report – A written document setting out a child's achievements at school during a fixed period of time.

Resources – Equipment used by teachers to aid the learning process.

Revenue expenditure – Expenditure on general running costs such as salaries, rates and fuel. *See also *capital expenditure.*

Rote learning – Learning off by heart, typically through repetition.

S1-S4 – Forms which need to be completed by schools as part of an *OFSTED inspection.

Scaffolding – Support provided to enable children to complete more complex tasks, typically by breaking down the task into simpler ones, or providing prompts that enable children to make step-by-step progress.

Scheme of work – A written document outlining lessons and *learning objectives within a particular *unit of work.

School achievement award – Direct grants from the government to schools to celebrate and reward successes and encourage further improvement. Most awards were given to schools where students' performance showed substantial improvement over time. About 30% of schools won awards each year, a typical *primary school getting £5,700 and a *secondary school £25,000. The scheme was phased out in 2003.

School action – Refers to measures taken by a school which are designed to help children with *special educational needs. School action equates to the provision of interventions that are additional to, or different from, those provided as part of the school's usual differentiated curriculum.

School action plus – Similar to *school action, but with the addition of a school request for help from external support services.

School adjudicator – Officials employed by the government to take decisions on *School Organisation Plans, individual proposals for change to school organisation, or issues relating to schools admission arrangements where it has not been possible to resolve the matter at a local level.

School-based assessment – A system where a child's progress is internally monitored and assessed in order to identify an individual need.

School causing concern – An official term to describe a school falling into one of the following categories:
- Requiring special measures
- With serious weaknesses
- Self- or *LEA categorisation as causing concern
- Low-attaining
- Underperforming

School-Centred Initial Teacher Training (SCITT) – The training of teachers in schools rather than in teacher training colleges. The government has recently encouraged this training route for new teachers, especially those who have come from another profession.

School Development Plan (SDP) – *See *School Improvement Plan.*

School facing challenging circumstances – A school in challenging circumstances where fewer than 25% of their students are achieving five or more grade A*-C grades in *GCSE or similar examinations.

School finance officer – *See *bursar.*

School fund – A fund which is maintained through voluntary contributions and fundraising activities, but is independent of the school's main finances.

School Improvement Plan (SIP) – A plan outlining an individual school's priorities over a period of time (commonly two to four years), usually with costings and details of monitoring strategies. Now often used in place of the term *school development plan.

School Library Association (SLA) – A membership organisation supporting all those committed to the promotion and development of school libraries and information literacy. www.sla.org.uk

School Library Service (SLS) – A service offered by an *LEA that replaces or enhances school libraries.

School Organisation Committee (SOC) A decision-making body at local level which votes on issues in an *LEA's *school organisation plan and other statutory proposals affecting education locally.

School Organisation Plan (SOP) – A plan prepared by an *LEA which provides a framework for decisions about the overall need to provide additional school places, or the need to remove existing school places, over a five year period.

Schools' Access Initiative (SAI) – A government scheme to provide funding to make mainstream schools more accessible to children with disabilities and *special educational needs.

Schools Music Association – A membership association supporting the work of music teachers.
www.schoolsmusic.org.uk

School Teachers' Review Body – A body set up in 1991 to examine and report on matters relating to the statutory conditions of employment of school teachers in England and Wales. It has a key role in determining pay settlements for teachers.

Secondary Heads Association (SHA) – The professional association for members of the *leadership group in *secondary schools and colleges. Headteachers, deputy headteachers and *assistant headteachers are eligible for SHA membership.
www.sha.org.uk

Secondary school – A school providing education to children in years 7 - 11, or in some cases years 7 - 13.

Secondment – The temporary transfer of a member of staff to another post. Experienced teachers are sometimes seconded to the *LEA to work in an advisory role.

Section 28 – A law which prohibited the promotion of homosexuality by teachers. It was repealed in July 2003.

Seed challenge fund – A government fund which enables schools to undertake building and accommodation-related projects by providing part funding toward the total costs of the scheme. The grant is intended to address the most pressing accommodation needs in schools.

Self-evaluation – A mechanism that allows schools to judge how effective they are in key areas of their work. Self-evaluations involve schools answering questions about their practice or giving scores that reflect their expertise in particular areas. The new

framework for *OFSTED inspections puts increased emphasis on the importance of self-evaluation.

Senior Management Team (SMT) – A senior management group in a school, usually comprising the headteacher, deputy headteacher(s) and other key personnel. The SMT takes day to day charge of running the school and makes key decisions on aspects of the school's provision.

Senior school – See *upper school.

Sensory difficulty – Any difficulty relating to the senses.

Serious weaknesses – A school is said to have serious weaknesses if, in the view of an OFSTED inspection team, it has significant weaknesses in one or more areas, but in general provides an acceptable standard of education overall. In such cases the inspection team makes detailed recommendations for how the school can improve in its report. The school will then be closely monitored for a period after the inspection to assess if it is making satisfactory progress in addressing issues in the action plan. If the problems are not resolved, it may be decided that the school must go into *special measures.

Set – See *setting.

Setting – Putting children into different groups for a particular subject, according to their ability in that subject.

Severe Communication Difficulties (SCD) – Communication difficulties which can present significant barriers to learning.

Severe Learning Difficulties (SLD) – Learning difficulties which can present significant barriers to learning.

Shared writing – The teaching method whereby a teacher asks for contributions from the whole class in constructing a piece of written work which is shared as it is devised.

Short course – A GCSE-level course which counts as half a full *GCSE.

Sixth-form college – An educational institution for 16 - 19 year-olds, taking students from several schools in any one area.

Society of Teachers in Business Education – A membership organisation which promotes the professional development of all those who work in business education. www.stbe.net

Society of Teachers of Speech and Drama – A membership organisation which aims to encourage good standards of teaching in speech and drama. www.stsd.org.uk

Special Educational Needs (SEN) – A child is described as having special educational needs if they are vulnerable to underachievement as a result of a specific barrier to learning. Many children with SEN have a physical, mental or learning disability that reduces their capacity to access the curriculum. Interventions are put in place in schools to help such children.

Special Educational Needs Co-ordinator (SENCO) – The member of staff responsible for arranging provision for children with *special educational needs.

Special Educational Needs & Disability Tribunal (SENDT) – An independent body to which parents/carers can appeal against decisions made by *LEAs about their children's education.

Special Educational Needs Support Service (SENSS) – An *LEA division which supports the provision of education for children with *special educational needs.

Specialist school (or college) – A school that has been successful under the government's *Specialist Schools Programme.

Specialist Schools Programme (SSP) – A government initiative to create, from existing secondary schools, schools that specialise in specific areas of the curriculum. Substantial additional funding is available over four years to schools that make successful bids, and find £50,000 in matched funding themselves from their local communities. The specialisms currently available are: business and enterprise, arts, engineering, languages, mathematics and computing, science, sports, and technology.

Specialist Teacher Assistant (STA) – A *teaching assistant who has undergone extensive additional training, leading to the award of the Specialist Teacher Assistant Certificate.

Special measures – A school is placed in special measures if it is found to be failing to provide an acceptable standard of education during an *OSFTED inspection.

Schools in special measures must prepare a detailed plan of action, with a timetable for when improvements will be achieved. The school will then be monitored for the next two years and re-inspected. If the school achieves the targets set out in its plan it is taken out of special measures. If it does not make acceptable progress, it could be closed down.

Special needs – See *Special Educational Needs*.

Special school – A school educating children with *special educational needs. Many of the children educated in special schools have *profound and multiple learning difficulties.

Specification – Another word for syllabus.

Specific learning difficulty (SpLD) – Used in some *LEAs in preference to *dyslexia.

Spelling, punctuation and grammar (SPG) – Every *GCSE examination now includes marks for children's spelling, punctuation and grammar.

Stakeholder – Any group or individual who has an interest in, or can affect the future of, the proposal being discussed.

Standard Attainment Test (SAT) – An assessment within the *National Curriculum composed of externally set tests.

Standard number – The number of children in each year group below which the *governing body cannot legally refuse admission.

Standards fund – An additional government funding stream that targets specific aspects of schools' provision through funding.

Standard Spending Assessment (SSA) – A notional calculation of what each local council needs to spend to provide a standard level of service, and an important part of the formula for distributing central government funds to councils. The calculation reflects the varying costs of providing services in each council area because of their different demographic, physical, economic and social characteristics.

Standing Advisory Council on Religious Education (SACRE) – The group that advises an *LEA on the provision of religious education in its schools. Every LEA is required by law to have such a group, which usually comprises local authority employees, members of religious bodies and teachers.

Starter – An initial activity with which a teacher begins a lesson, and the first part of the *four-part lesson structure. Starters are designed to engage interest and arouse curiosity, providing an effective basis for the lesson to follow.

Statement bank – A list of phrases used by teachers to speed up the preparation of students' reports. Many statement banks allow teachers to select code numbers for particular statements from a list, which are then assembled into a report electronically by *support staff.

Statement of special education need – A statutory document, drawn up by an *LEA in consultation with parents/carers, that describes a child's *special educational needs and how they are met. The process of making the assessment is known as statementing.

State school – See *maintained school.

Statutory provision – Provision by schools as required by an Act of Parliament or other legislation; for example all education of students towards formal examinations.

Statutory school age – The period from the beginning of the term following a child's fifth birthday until the leaving date following his or her 16th birthday.

Strategic plan – A school document establishing priorities for curriculum development, staffing and site over a period of time, typically five years.

Stream – See *streaming*.

Streaming – A type of school organisation where children are placed into groups according to their ability and stay in these groups for most of their lessons.

Student-centred learning – Education which, rather than focusing on the teacher, encourages active engagement from the student in the learning process.

Subject co-ordinator – A member of staff responsible for the management of a particular subject area, usually in a *primary school. Sometimes also called a *subject leader.

Subject leader – A member of staff, usually in a *secondary school, responsible for the management of the curriculum in a particular subject area. Also called a *head of department*.

Summative assessment – Assessment taking place at the end of a course, which aims to identify the student's level of attainment. *See also *formative assessment*.

Supply teacher – A teacher employed to cover for staff absence, usually through a company providing this service such as a teacher supply agency.

Support Society for Children of High Intelligence, The – A charity supporting the specific needs of very able children. The services offered include assessment of very able children, counselling and support, and the provision of Saturday classes. www.chi-charity.org.uk

Support staff – Any non-teaching staff who assist with the running of the school.

Support teacher – See **Teaching Assistant*.

Sure Start – The government's programme to deliver the best start in life for every child, bringing together early education, childcare and health, and family support. www.surestart.gov.uk

Sustainable development – See **Education for Sustainable Development*.

SWOT analysis (strengths, weaknesses, opportunities, threats – A management tool for issue analysis or decision-making.

Syllabus – A written summary of a course.

Synoptic assessment – Assessment which requires students to show they have understood how different elements of the course relate to each other.

Talented – A child is defined by the *DfES as talented if they are very able in art, music, physical education or performing arts. The word has also been used more generally in the past by teachers to refer to an able child. Talented children have come under the spotlight as part of the Gifted and Talented Strand of *Excellence in Cities. *See also *gifted*.

Target setting – The setting of agreed academic or personal targets with children in order to give them appropriate goals and challenges. Target setting has become a key way to improve student performance in recent years.

Teacher assessment – Assessment carried out by the teacher, as opposed to in external examinations.

Teacher-centred education – Refers to a teacher-led model of education rather than one where active student participation is encouraged. *Compare with *child-centred education*.

Teacher Contact Ratio (TCR) – The proportion of the school day when secondary teachers are in charge of classes, as opposed to marking work or preparing lessons.

TeacherNet – A *DfES internet gateway to the world of education for teachers, classroom assistants and headteachers. Information is included on policy developments, new practices in teaching and learning, management and professional development and educational research. www.teachernet.gov.uk

Teachers Online Project (TOP) – A website which demonstrates the benefits of the internet in

improving classroom practice, school administration and management. www.ictadvice.org.uk

Teacher Support Line – A service for teachers offering information, support or short-term counselling to help them cope with the demands of teaching. Telephone or email enquiries can be made. Tel. 08000 562 561 www.teacherline.org.uk

Teacher Training Agency (TTA) – The government agency which supports the recruitment of teachers in England and Wales. The TTA provides information and advice for prospective teachers, including details of the various training routes. www.tta.gov.uk

Teaching as a Second Career (TASC) – Refers to individuals who enter teaching following employment in other fields.

T

Teaching Assistant (TA) – The *DfES's preferred term for any member of staff who aids the teacher by working with groups of children inside the classroom. Historically, people who carry out this role have been known as non-teaching assistants, classroom support assistants, language support assistants, learning support assistants and support assistants.

Teaching style – The particular teaching method used by a teacher. Studies of the most effective teachers show that they vary their teaching style to appeal to children with different *learning styles.

Team teaching – The process by which two or more teachers join together to teach a lesson. Team teaching is common during teacher training and enables teaching skills to be acquired in a supportive environment.

Technology College – See *specialist school and *Specialist Schools Programme.

Technology Colleges Trust (TCT) – The body which manages the *Specialist Schools Programme on behalf of the *DfES. Also known as Specialist Schools Trust. www.tctrust.org.uk

Technology Schools Initiative (TSI) – A government initiative, launched in 1991, to promote the first *specialist schools.

Terminal assessment/examination – An assessment which takes place at the end of a course.

Tertiary college – A college for young people over the age of 16 that combines the functions of a *sixth-form college and a *further education college by offering a wide range of academic and *vocational qualifications.

Thinking skills – Skills which promote effective thinking. The government has identified five thinking skills as part of the *National Curriculum: information-processing skills, reasoning skills, enquiry skills, creative thinking skills and evaluation skills.

Thoughtshower(ing) – The process of thinking through an issue or question by generating as many potential ideas or solutions as possible. Some people believe the term

brainstorm(ing), which refers to the same process, should now be avoided because a brainstorm is a mental disturbance from which epileptics suffer.

Threshold – The level above which teachers can access higher pay by proving their competence through *performance management.

Threshold assessment – An assessment teachers undergo when they wish to move on to the *upper pay scale. This is normally only possible when they reach the top of the standard pay scale at point M6.

Tier – Many *GCSEs are now tiered according to their level of difficulty, with foundation, intermediate and higher tiers available. Students are entered for one of these tiers by their teacher.

Times Educational Supplement (TES) – The principal newspaper for teachers in the UK, issued weekly on a Friday.

Tracking – The monitoring of a child or child group to determine their progress.

Trainee heads scheme – A government scheme to place experienced deputy headteachers who have potential for headship, in good schools facing challenging circumstances.

Training day – A day held in term time during which the school is closed to children, but staff undertake training, or work on whole school development issues.

Transition – Usually refers to the time when a child moves from primary to secondary school between year 6 and 7. There has been widespread concern that children are vulnerable to suffering what has been termed a 'learning loss' during this time, and a range of summer schools and other interventions have been put in place to counteract this.

Truancy – A situation where a student deliberately misses school without good reason. *See also *authorised absence and *unauthorised absence.*

Tutor group – A group of children, usually in the same *year group, who register together with a *form tutor during morning and afternoon *registration.

Twilight – Usually refers to training or meetings which take place after the school day, typically between 4 and 6 pm.

Unauthorised absence – Absence which is not considered legitimate by the headteacher, and which is recorded in a school's truancy record. *See also* *authorised absence*.

Underachiever – A child whose academic performance does not reach what is reasonably expected given the child's perceived ability. Typically this leads to poorer results than the child is capable of in tests and examinations.

Unique Pupil Number (UPN) – A number allocated by the government to each child in an English *state school. It is an identifier for use in the educational context during a child's school career and is subject to data protection restrictions.

Unit of work – A smaller unit within a *scheme of work.

Universities and Colleges Admissions Service (UCAS) – The UK central organisation through which applications are processed for entry to *higher education, providing information and services to prospective students. www.ucas.ac.uk

University of the First Age (UFA) – A charity working in partnership with schools and communities to extend learning beyond the school day. It was founded in 1996 in Birmingham and now works nationally, using innovative brain-based approaches to increase learning potential and raise achievement. www.ufa.org.uk

Upper pay scale – The pay scale that teachers move on to, having successfully crossed the *threshold.

Upper school – A school taking children who have left *middle school age 12 or 13. Some secondary schools also use the term to describe years 10 and 11. *See also *lower school.

Vertical group – A class (usually in a *primary school) made up of children of different age groups. In *secondary schools children are sometimes placed in vertical tutor groups.

Virement – The process of transferring funds from one expenditure heading to another.

Virtual Teacher Centre (VTC) – A government website providing support materials for primary and secondary teaching in all areas of the curriculum, plus information on school management. A principal feature of the site is the ability for teachers to share ideas and good practice electronically, and submit content to be considered for *Curriculum Online. www.vtc.ngfl.gov.uk

Value added – The additional educational gain that a school gives to a child or group of children. The government recently introduced value added measures into schools' performance tables to provide a more realistic comparison between schools.

Visual learner – A learner who prefers to learn through seeing (sometimes called the visual channel). *See also *learning style.*

Vocational course – A course tailored to a specific profession, rather than being purely academic in nature.

Vocational education – Education geared to the world of work.

Vocational GCSE – A qualification usually taken at age 16 and linked closely to a specific profession. Vocational GCSEs are replacing *GNVQs.

Voluntary Aided (VA) school – A school receiving financial support from a voluntary body, usually a church. Such schools often have a strong religious ethos and employ teachers who are in sympathy with the ethos of a church school.

Voluntary Controlled (VC) school – A school receiving funding from the *LEA, but which is owned by a voluntary body, frequently with religious connections.

Voluntary School – *See *Voluntary Controlled school.*

Welsh Joint Education Committee (WJEC) – The Welsh examination board whose syllabuses and exams are available to English schools.

Withdrawal – The removal of children with particular needs from *primary school classes, and from specified subjects in *secondary schools, for additional one-to-one or group support. *In-class support is used in many schools in preference to withdrawal.

Work experience (WEX) – The period of time (usually one to two weeks) a child spends outside school, experiencing the world of work. During this time the child carries out a particular job or range of jobs, more or less as a regular employee would. It may take place any time after the Easter break in year 10.

Workforce remodelling agreement – A document signed by the government and teacher unions which sets out workplace reforms that will enable teachers to concentrate on teaching. One of the key features was the removal of many administrative duties from teachers' responsibilities.

Work-related learning – Learning carried out by children during *work experience placements, or during alternative courses taken by children who have been disapplied *(See *disapplication)* from the *National Curriculum.

Writing frame – A printed framework to help children write more effectively, usually involving prompts and other devices to promote thinking and planning.

Year group – Refers to all the children in a specific chronological year at school, starting in year 1 (age 5 - 6) and ending when they leave school in year 11 (age 15 - 16) or year 13 (age 17 - 18). Year R refers to reception classes, in which children are placed before beginning year 1. *See *Key Stages (1-4).*

Year R – *See *year group.*

Year 11 Information system (YELLIS) – A *value added monitoring system that identifies a wide range of performance indicators for children aged 14 - 16. The *value added approach allows schools to make a fair comparison of the progress made by students who take a formal test with that made by all other students taking the test nationally. Also sometimes called Years of Late Secondary Information System. (YELSIS) www.yellis.cem.dur.ac.uk/

Youth offending team – A local government department responsible for reducing criminal activity among young people.

AAN	–	Approved Admission Number
ACE	–	Advisory Centre for Education
ACS	–	Average Class Size
ACT	–	Association for Citizenship Teaching
ADD	–	Attention Deficit Disorder
ADHD	–	Attention Deficit Hyperactivity Disorder
ALIS	–	Advanced Level Information System
ALP	–	Association of Learning Providers
ALT	–	Association for Learning Technology
AMP	–	Asset Management Plan
APL	–	Accreditation of Prior Learning
APS	–	Assisted Places Scheme
AQA	–	Assessment and Qualifications Alliance
ARR	–	Assessment, Recording and Reporting
ASB	–	Aggregated Schools' Budget
ASE	–	Association for Science Education
AST	–	Advanced Skills Teacher
ASVCE	–	Advanced Subsidiary Vocational Certificate of Education
AT	–	Attainment Target

ATL	–	Association of Teachers and Lecturers
ATM	–	Association for Teachers of Mathematics
AVA	–	Audio Visual Aids
AVCE	–	Advanced Vocational Certificate of Education
AWPU	–	Age Weighted Pupil Unit
BDP	–	Bursar Development Programme
BECTA	–	British Educational Communications and Technology Agency
BEd	–	Bachelor of Education
BELMAS	–	British Educational Leadership Management and Administration Society
BSA	–	Basic Skills Agency
BSP	–	Behaviour Support Plan
CAL	–	Computer Assisted Learning
CAME	–	Cognitive Acceleration through Maths Education

CASE	–	Campaign for State Education
CASE	–	Cognitive Acceleration through Science Education
CAT	–	Cognitive Ability Test
CATE	–	Cognitive Acceleration through Technology Education
CBDS	–	Common Basic Data Set
CCT	–	Compulsory Competitive Tendering
CDC	–	Curriculum Development Centre
CFE	–	College of Further Education
CHE	–	College of Higher Education
CLC	–	City Learning Centre
COP	–	Code of Practice
CPD	–	Continuing Professional Development
CPS	–	Common Pay Spine
CRE	–	Campaign for Real Education
CSA	–	Classroom Support Assistant
CTC	–	City Technology College
DART	–	Directed Activity Related to Text

DDA	–	Disability Discrimination Act
DEC	–	Development Education Centre
DfES	–	Department for Education and Skills
EAB	–	Examinations Appeals Board
EAL	–	English as an Additional Language
EAZ	–	Education Action Zone
EBD	–	Emotional and Behavioural Difficulty/Disorder
EBP	–	Education Business Partnership
EDP	–	Educational Development Plan
EiC	–	Excellence in Cities
ELC	–	eLearning Credit
EMA	–	Education Maintenance Allowance
EO	–	Education Otherwise
EOTAS	–	Education Other Than At School
ESD	–	Education for Sustainable Development
ESO	–	Education Supervision Order
EVC	–	Educational Visits Co-ordinator
EWO	–	Education Welfare Officer
EWS	–	Education Welfare Service
FE	–	Further Education
FSP	–	Foundation Stage Profile
FT	–	Full-time
FTE	–	Full-time equivalent
GCE	–	General Certificate of Education
GCSE	–	General Certificate of Secondary Education
GMS	–	Grant Maintained School
GNVQ	–	General National Vocational Qualification
GTC	–	General Teaching Council
HE	–	Higher Education
HEADLAMP	–	Headteachers' Leadership and Management Programme
HIP	–	Headteacher Induction Programme
HLTA	–	Higher Level Teaching Assistant

HMI	–	Her Majesty's Inspector (of schools)
HOD	–	Head of Department
HOF	–	Head of Faculty
HOY	–	Head of Year
HSA	–	Home-School Agreement
IB	–	International Baccalaureate
IBP	–	Individual Behaviour Plan
ICT	–	Information and Communication Technology
IEP	–	Individual Education Plan
IiP	–	Investors in People
INSET	–	In-Service Education and Training
IQ	–	Intelligence Quotient
ISB	–	Individual Schools' Budget
IT	–	Information Technology
ITT	–	Initial Teacher Training
KS	–	Key Stage
LEA	–	Local Education Authority
LMS	–	Local Management of Schools
LMSS	–	Local Management of Special Schools
LPSH	–	Leadership Programme for Serving Headteachers
LRC	–	Learning Resource Centre
LSA	–	Learning Support Assistant
LSB	–	Local Schools' Budget
LSC	–	Learning and Skills Council
LSU	–	Learning Support Unit
LTL	–	Learning Through Landscapes
MARRA	–	Monitoring, Assessment, Recording, Reporting and Accountability
MFL	–	Modern Foreign Language(s)
Mid-Yis	–	Middle Years Information System
MLD	–	Moderate Learning Difficulties
NACE	–	National Association for Able Children in Education
NAGC	–	National Association for Gifted Children
NAGTY	–	National Academy for Gifted and Talented Youth
NAHT	–	National Association of Head Teachers

NAME	–	National Association for Music Educators
NAPE	–	National Association for Primary Education
NASEN	–	National Association for Special Educational Needs
NASUWT	–	National Association of Schoolmasters Union of Women Teachers
NATE	–	National Association for Teachers of English
NBA	–	National Bursars Association
NC	–	National Curriculum
NCSL	–	National College for School Leadership
NFER	–	National Foundation for Educational Research
NGfL	–	National Grid for Learning
NLS	–	National Literacy Strategy
NNS	–	National Numeracy Strategy
NOR	–	Number on/of Roll
NPFA	–	National Playing Fields Association
NPQH	–	National Professional Qualification for Headship
NQT	–	Newly Qualified Teacher
NTA	–	Non-Teaching Assistant
NUT	–	National Union of Teachers
OCR	–	Oxford Cambridge and RSA examinations
OEA	–	Outdoor Education Adviser
OFSTED	–	Office for Standards in Education
PAL	–	Published Admissions Limit
PANDA	–	Performance and Assessment Data
PAS	–	Psychology and Assessment Service
PAT	–	Professional Association of Teachers
PC	–	Parental Contribution
PFI	–	Private Finance Initiative
PGCE	–	Postgraduate Certificate of Education
PIC	–	Pre-Inspection Commentary

PIPS	–	Performance Indicators in Primary Schools
PIVATS	–	Performance Indicators for Value Added Target Setting
PLASC	–	Pupil Level Annual Schools' Census
PMLD	–	Profound and Multiple Learning Difficulties
POS	–	Programme of Study
PPS	–	Parent Partnership Scheme
PRU	–	Pupil Referral Unit
PSHCE	–	Personal, Social, Health and Citizenship Education
PSHE	–	Personal, Social and Health Education
PT	–	Part-time
PTA	–	Parent Teacher Association
PTE	–	Part-time Equivalent
PTR	–	Pupil/Teacher Ratio
QCA	–	Qualifications and Curriculum Authority
QTS	–	Qualified Teacher Status
REACH	–	Record of Achievement
RgI/RI	–	Registered Inspector
ROA	–	Record of Achievement
SACRE	–	Standing Advisory Council on Religious Education
SAI	–	Schools' Access Initiative
SAT	–	Standard Assessment Test
SCD	–	Severe Communication Difficulties
SCITT	–	School-Centred Initial Teacher Training
SDP	–	School Development Plan
SEN	–	Special Educational Needs
SENCO	–	Special Educational Needs Co-ordinator
SENDT	–	Special Educational Needs & Disability Tribunal
SENSS	–	Special Educational Needs Support Services
SHA	–	Secondary Heads Association
SIP	–	School Improvement Plan
SLA	–	School Library Association

SLD	–	Severe Learning Difficulties
SLS	–	School Library Service
SMT	–	Senior Management Team
SNSS	–	Special Needs Support Service
SOC	–	School Organisation Committee
SOP	–	School Organisation Plan
SPG	–	Spelling, Punctuation and Grammar
SpLD	–	Specific Learning Difficulty
SSA	–	Standard Spending Assessment
SSP	–	Specialist Schools Programme
STA	–	Specialist Teacher Assistant
TA	–	Teaching Assistant
TASC	–	Teaching as a Second Career
TCR	–	Teacher Contact Ratio
TCT	–	Technology Colleges Trust
TES	–	Times Educational Supplement
TOP	–	Teachers Online Project
TSI	–	Technology Schools Initiative
TTA	–	Teacher Training Agency
UCAS	–	Universities and Colleges Admissions Services
UFA	–	University of the First Age
UPN	–	Unique Pupil Number
VA	–	Voluntary Aided
VC	–	Voluntary Controlled
VI	–	Visually Impaired
VTC	–	Virtual Teacher Centre
WEX	–	Work Experience
WJEC	–	Welsh Joint Education Committee
YELLIS	–	Year 11 Information System
YELSIS	–	Years of Late Secondary Information System (See YELLIS)

About the author

Brin Best BSc, PGCE, FRGS, FMA, MCIJ is managing director of Innovation *for* Education Ltd, an education training, publishing and consultancy company based in Yorkshire. He has fulfilled a wide variety of roles within schools and local education authorities, and writes and speaks widely on education issues. Brin has been associated with the compilation of a number of jargon busters, and feels passionately about the need to demystify the language surrounding educational issues. He is a member of the Institute of Journalists and is the series consultant for the Teachers' Pocketbooks.

He can be contacted at: Innovation *for* Education Ltd, 6 Manor Square, Otley, LS21 3AP.
Tel. +44 (0) 1943 466994   Fax +44 (0) 1943 465550
office@innovation4education.co.uk www.innovation4education.co.uk

Bibliography

Butt, G. (2000)
The Continuum Guide to Geography Education
Continuum

Statham, J., Mackinnon, D. and Cathcart, H. (1989)
The Education Factfile
Hodder and Stoughton

Capel, S., Leask, M., Turner, T. (1999)
Learning to Teach in the Secondary School
Routledge

Order Form

Your details

Name _____

Position _____

School _____

Address _____

_____

_____

Telephone _____

Fax _____

E-mail _____

VAT No. (EC only) _____

Your Order Ref _____

Please send me:

		No. copies
A-Z of Educational Terms	Pocketbook	☐
_____	Pocketbook	☐
_____	Pocketbook	☐
_____	Pocketbook	☐
_____	Pocketbook	☐

Order by Post

Teachers' Pocketbooks

Laurel House, Station Approach
Alresford, Hants. SO24 9JH UK

Order by Phone, Fax or Internet
Telephone: +44 (0)1962 735573
Facsimile: +44 (0)1962 733637
E-mail: sales@teacherspocketbooks.co.uk
Web: www.teacherspocketbooks.co.uk